The Truth (As I See It)

A Former DA Speaks Out on Sex, Drugs,
Religion and Other Hot-button Issues

James L. Sepulveda

iUniverse, Inc.
New York   Bloomington

iUniverse books may be ordered through booksellers or by contacting:

iUniverse
1663 Liberty Drive
Bloomington, IN 47403
www.iuniverse.com
1-800-Authors (1-800-288-4677)

Because of the dynamic nature of the Internet, any Web addresses or
links contained in this book may have changed since publication and
may no longer be valid. The views expressed in this work are solely those
of the author and do not necessarily reflect the views of the publisher,
and the publisher hereby disclaims any responsibility for them.

ISBN: 978-1-4401-6269-5 (sc)
ISBN: 978-1-4401-6265-7 (ebook)

Printed in the United States of America

iUniverse rev. date: 9/14/2009

Dedicated to my father, George Sepulveda, who was my inspiration in life and the one who taught me to always seek and speak the truth; to Neale Donald Walsch, whose *Conversations with God* books taught me to really listen on all levels for God's guidance; and to my spiritual Father, whom I now realize is always there in all ways. I only have to listen with my soul.

Get wisdom, get understanding;
do not forget my words or swerve from them.
Do not forsake wisdom, and she will protect you;
love her and she will watch over you.
Wisdom is supreme; therefore get wisdom.
Though it cost you all you have, get understanding.
Esteem her, and she will exalt you;
embrace her, and she will honor you.
She will set a garland of grace on your head
and present you with a crown of splendor.

Proverbs 4: 5-9

Contents

Preface

Who the heck am I and why am I writing a book about "truth?" As to why, there are two reasons. The first reason is out of frustration at the human condition. If you really look at human progress over the last ten thousand plus years, it is pretty darn depressing. Oh, yes—we have made tremendous strides technologically. But how about sociologically? We still have the same mindless wars, racial hatred, religious intolerance, philosophical intolerance, greed, envy, subjugation of others, needless violence, poverty and hunger, and on and on. As a species, sociologically speaking, we continue to repeat the same mistakes over and over and over. Strip away our technology, and in many ways we have not progressed much as a species. And it all seems so senseless. We should be smart enough to know better. We should be smart enough to learn from the past and progress to a higher and more enlightened state. There seem to be so many "elephants in the room" that we routinely ignore, tiptoe around, and fail to acknowledge. Yet if we were able to acknowledge, accept, and deal with these "elephants" or—as I call them—truths, the world might just be a much better place. My concern about the human condition was one of my primary motivations.

The second reason may sound bizarre to some but it is my truth. Several years ago, I started making notes about things I saw that didn't make sense from a logical perspective. I had a vague notion about putting my thoughts in book form but never really followed up. A few months ago, I was hiking in the mountains above Lake Tahoe. I was by myself and it was a beautiful sunny day. In fact, it was December 10, 2008. When I hike by myself, I love to commune with nature and with God. That day I kept hearing the same message over and over—"Write your book." So I did.

Who am I to lecture anyone or philosophize about the human condition? Am I some genius or prophet? Heck, no! I am just an average guy. But maybe that is why I am qualified. I am not so smart as to make things complicated and I am not so dumb as to miss the obvious. What I do have is a wealth of experience in dealing with people. I was a criminal lawyer for over thirty-two years and dealt with every kind of person imaginable from the very best of us to the very worst of us and pretty much everyone else in between. I have dealt with people of all races, many different ethnicities, rich, poor, very smart, very dumb, humble, arrogant, powerful, and submissive. I had dealings with all levels of our various governments and all levels of government officials. I dealt with disputes of almost every imaginable kind from the petty to the ones leading to homicide.

I don't know if all my experience makes me an expert on the human condition but I sure have observed, both directly and vicariously, just about everything that human beings do to one another, both good and bad. One thing I have noticed over and over is that people do not and will not admit certain things publicly, but off the record they will admit to seeing the elephant in the room. As I have always considered myself a problem solver, I wanted to try to expose these elephants. Maybe that will help all of us face the truth, accept the truth, and deal with the truth. And then maybe that will help us all be better people.

Chapter 1

The Truth about Labels

Have you ever asked yourself why we can't all just get along? One of the reasons is our addiction to labels. Humans have a tendency to want to shorten everything—like names. Have you ever noticed that most everyone is identified by a shortened name or initials? Notice how common acronyms are? We want to make things short and easy to identify. Since life has gotten more and more complex, we need to simplify things so that we can more easily cope. It takes too much time to actually think about and analyze something, so we just stick a label on it. It makes it so much faster to categorize things that way. The problem is that labels are generally meaningless because they all mean different things to different people! Therefore, the use of labels often leads to misunderstandings, and then to friction, and then to God knows what.

Barack Obama is a "liberal." What does that mean? To some, that is a compliment. To others, that is the worst thing you can say about someone. We all have our own individual definition for that label. But because no one's definition of that term is exactly alike, the label is in reality meaningless. What do the terms conservative or liberal actually tell you about a person? The truth is those terms tell you absolutely *nothing* about the person. Yet think of all the labels we use in everyday life. Think of religious labels, like Jewish, Muslim, Catholic, Protestant, Baptist, agnostic, atheist, sinner, holy-roller, evangelist, spiritualist, and the list goes on and on. But the truth is that there is only one way to find out about any person's spirituality—that is to talk with that person and have a meaningful discourse about the subject. People's beliefs are like fingerprints, DNA, and snowflakes—no two are exactly alike. To judge someone based upon a label is really an act of ignorance. You are quite simply guessing with no knowledge upon which to base a guess.

Think of the other labels we use. How often have you heard a politician say that we need to tax the "rich?" What does that mean? Who are the rich? Does the term mean anyone with more assets than you? Does it mean inherited money or just income? And why is being rich considered derogatory? Aren't we all in a capitalist economy supposed to strive to be rich? Why are lotteries so popular? Why is gambling so popular? Being "rich" doesn't seem to be so bad when a politician is hosting a ten-thousand-dollars-a-plate dinner. Basically, it is a meaningless hot-button label used to pacify those who are angry that someone else has more than they do.

What other hot button labels are used to try to influence people, either for or against something or someone? Activist, bleeding heart, fanatic, heretic, hawk, dove, gun lover, big spender, miser, pro-life, pro-choice, macho, woman's libber, intellectual, socialist, communist, elitist, middle class, third world, big business, corporate, small town, country, redneck, sophisticated, classy, classless, fat, thin, fat cat, jock—you could add hundreds, maybe thousands, of other general labels we use to describe people. That is not to say that a label cannot ever tell you something about a person. Obviously, some labels give you some clue about a person. Probably someone described as African American is not going to have white skin. Calling someone pro-life tells you something about his belief about abortion, although even here there are a myriad of shades and the label tells you nothing about where on the spectrum of pro-life beliefs this person is. A person who is macho is probably male. But really look at the label. What does it tell you about the heart of that person? Can you tell whether the person is kind or mean to his family, thoughtful to others or thoughtless, a good worker or lazy and non-productive, smart or stupid, spiritual or not, compassionate or hateful? Some bleeding hearts are mean and nasty. And there are gun-loving hawks who are as loving and compassionate as anyone. Once again, the only way to truly and accurately judge another person is by actually getting to know him or her and having a dialogue. We have all been forced into situations where we are compelled to deal with someone that we think we will hate; once we put our preconceived notions aside, we often end up really liking that person instead. Almost everyone has some good and some bad. Very few of us are saints and very few of us are truly evil. We would all be better served if we recognized labels for just what they are—broad generalizations that have little or no meaning when applied to specific individuals.

Who labels people? And why? Labeling things and people has become a way of life for politicians, the media, and those with a "cause." It is a simplistic way to convey a message. Politicians and advocates also use a number of hot-button labels to rally people to their causes or against some other person or cause. This tactic is simple and doesn't require much explanation. It is especially effective in today's climate of politics by sound-bite. The real advantage is that you really don't have to have a brain in your head; even a parrot can be taught to throw out some jingoistic, meaningless banalities. Even though advocates know or should know that different folks will interpret the label different ways, they don't really care as long as they feel they are reaping some political benefit. Because people tend to assume that everyone else uses the same definitions that they use for these labels, people go away satisfied, feeling that they are part of a larger group that shares the same beliefs.

The media is also guilty of labeling. Why? Because the media is tasked with presenting a lot of complex information in a story condensed into one to two minutes. To adequately report the news, the news shows would have to be several hours long. To report all nuances and sides of a story fairly, a reporter might need many minutes or even an hour or more. Even though the print media has more time and space, even a newspaper or magazine story is limited to telling only a small portion of what actually transpired. Editors decide what is important and not important. They are really the ultimate censors of what we read and hear. So, much like the politician and the advocate, they find it is easy and fast to use labels. You don't need to explain or go into detail. And, like any person telling a story, reporters can use the labels to influence the reader without ever having to establish a factual basis for the report or opinions expressed. Based upon my experience with the media, most stories are, at best, factually incomplete and misleading and, at worst, downright untrue. Almost anyone involved in an incident that received substantial publicity will tell you that it is disconcerting to read or see something in the news about that event. You wonder if they are talking about the same incident! I have seen stories describing events at which I was personally present and generally have been aghast at the inaccuracies and untruths that were reported. In this modern world, perception has a way of becoming reality. It is astounding that people actually swallow, hook, line, and sinker, everything they see and read in the media. Once reported, no matter how inaccurately, the story becomes the truth.

Unfortunately, we as a people are so used to dealing with labels that we tend to accept them at face value. The sad truth is that we assume that everyone else sees the world the same way we do. That is why you see people who seemingly agree on an issue that has only been vaguely described by a label discover that, in fact, they do not see eye to eye once they actually sit down and have a dialogue about their views. The use and acceptance of labels is one of the biggest causes of mistrust and misunderstanding in society today. That is true in our personal relationships, homes, businesses, local communities, state and federal governments, and internationally. People talk but do not listen. People do not really seek to understand what the speaker is saying. We need to be critical listeners who question labels and assumptions and undocumented conclusions. Speakers need to be held accountable for what they say and pressed to explain and define their terminology. If a speaker is too lazy, too pressed for time, or just can't explain the factual basis for his or her views, maybe we should at least view the statements with some cynicism and distrust. Unfortunately, people tend to hear what they want to hear and tend only to be critical of views that do not seem to be in line with their own.

So let us explore some examples of preconceived notions and labels. Picture in your mind the following: an Irish, Catholic, pro-life, macho man. Because all our experience comes to us through our senses, and because no two humans have exactly the same sensory abilities or experiences, each human being that has ever existed has had a unique life experience. Therefore, no two human beings will perceive everything exactly the same. There is nothing wrong with that. The problem is that we tend to assume that the rest of the world sees the world through our eyes and make judgments accordingly. We should acknowledge our uniqueness and seek to understand the views and perceptions of others. It really is okay that there are different perspectives. Life would probably easier, but a lot more boring, if everyone saw the world exactly the same way. But labels tend to make us lazy; we believe that there are not different views. Labels tend to offer a false comfort that others think just like us. The truth is that *no one* thinks just like you! No one ever has and no one ever will.

Okay—to our example. Do you have the picture of an Irish, Catholic, pro-life, macho man in your mind? What is Irish to you? Do you have to be born in Ireland? Do you just have to have an Irish name? Many slaves were given names by their owners and hence many descendants of slaves have Irish names! If your great-grandfather was one-quarter Irish, is that enough? Do you understand that what may be Irish to you may not be Irish to someone else?

What is a Catholic? Do you have to go to church? Do you have to believe in all the Catholic dogma? Is it enough if you were forced to go to Catholic school or church as a kid and have not gone back since? Is it enough if you go to church on Easter even if you otherwise don't know about, care about, or even follow Catholic dogma? What if you believe the dogma but never go to church and have never been baptized? Depending on their own life experiences, different people will define the label Catholic differently.

What does pro-life mean? Does it mean you oppose all abortions no matter what? Does it mean that you only oppose some abortions but that those done to protect a mother's life or in cases of rape or incest are okay? Does it mean that you believe that anyone who performs an abortion should be hunted down and murdered? Does it mean that you personally would not have an abortion but you believe that it is an individual choice of conscience? A very broad spectrum of beliefs can fall under that label.

And what is macho? To some, the term means a man who likes challenging outdoor activity. To others, it means someone who mistreats and/or disrespects women. Maybe it is someone who believes in traditionally defined roles for men and women but treats women with deference and respect. Maybe it just means a braggart. The term evokes strong emotional responses but is rather meaningless because it can mean such different things to different people.

So now what does your Irish, Catholic, pro-life, macho man look like? There are almost an endless number of combinations and permutations. This could be one terrific, sensitive, loving, spiritual man or a real callous, mean-spirited jerk. How can anyone legitimately judge this person without spending some time with him and getting to really know him? The danger of labels is that we categorize and sort people without ever really knowing them. It is convenient. It is easy. It doesn't require effort. It doesn't require knowledge. Any idiot can do it. And it helps us shape the world to be what we want it to be rather than having to deal with reality. Therein lies the rub. Labels are generalizations. Generalizations are by definition not specific. But each person is a specific, unique being. Therefore, labels, by their very nature, distort the truth and lead to misunderstanding, hatred, and mistrust. We as a people will always use labels, but we need to be more cognizant about applying generalizations to specific individuals.

Chapter 2

The Truth about Men

It's funny how often you see or hear the truth alluded to. The book *Men Are From Mars and Women Are From Venus,* by John Gray, certainly describes the differences but, by putting things in psychological terms, Gray avoids some of the more blunt truths. A country song, *The Truth about Men,* is closer to the naked truth but softens the blow through the use of music and humor. Despite the obvious physical differences, and the myriad of psychological differences (and there are a lot of good books discussing these aspects), there is one subject that is rarely directly discussed. Sex.

Now, my opinions and experiences apply to heterosexual men. It may be that gay men feel the same but as I have no experience in that area, I am not qualified to offer any insight.

In my experience, women mature pretty much on a linear level. That is to say, their bodies and their psyches mature at a certain rate of progression. The rate obviously varies from woman to woman, but a woman in her forties is different in mind and body from that same woman in her twenties. The whole of her moves on as she experiences life. For men, although their bodies certainly mature at some linear rate, only part of their mind follows suit. For all men that I have ever known, part of their mental development stopped at around age sixteen. That part continues to exist but never progresses past a certain level of immaturity. Freud would call it the libido. It is the part that focuses a lot on women and sex.

The book *Clan of the Cave Bear*, by Jean Auel, presented a fascinating look at the primitive caveman. In the book, the traditional caveman took any woman he wanted whenever he wanted. Right then and there, part of man's brain stopped evolving. It liked it there! And thousands of years later, that part still exists in most men. It can be a bigger and more prominent part in some men's brain than in others, but it still exists, and although we deny it (especially to girlfriends and wives), it plays a pivotal role in almost all heterosexual relationships.

What is every man's fantasy? It is to be able to have sex with whomever he wants whenever he wants. And the more the merrier. Most men know they are not great lovers, but they would like someone to at least pretend they are. Every man looks at virtually every woman he sees or meets and evaluates her as a potential sexual partner. For you sickos, I am not talking about mothers, daughters, little kids, etc. I am talking about women between the ages of eighteen to however old your tastes run. It can be a fellow worker, a waitress where you eat, your boss, your friends' wives, your wife's friends, or strangers on the street. For most men, their innate, instinctive thought process when seeing or meeting a woman is to think of her first in sexual terms. Sorry to spill the beans, but this is the God's honest truth, and if any man, when confronted by his wife or girlfriend, denies this, he is lying. It may be a good idea to lie, by the way, for self-protection. But if both sexes acknowledged the truth, relationships might improve because there would be more understanding. Now, please understand, it is not that we necessarily want to initially just think of women in sexual terms, it is just that we can't help it. It is a natural and ingrained part of us. Just as women tend to have a motherly instinct, men have an inbred instinct to mate and perpetuate the species. What, after all, is the most basic primal instinct? Survival! Every creature that has ever existed has fought tooth and nail to ensure its individual survival and the survival of its kind. Part of surviving as a species is to procreate. Sorry—but that is the way that nature made us. Maybe we will outgrow this someday, but the truth is that we have not made much progress over the last tens of thousands of years.

The inevitable question arises—what about love? The truth? Can you handle the truth? The truth is that love has nothing to do with it. For men, there is a big difference between love and sex. Women tend to associate love and sex. Those terms and feelings are an integral part of an emotional bond. For men, there is emotion in love but sex is an act of self-gratification requiring no emotional investment whatsoever. Love and sex are not necessarily related topics for men. What does that mean? Can you love someone yet fantasize about having sex with someone else? Absolutely! I have the greatest wife in the world. I literally would not trade her for any other woman on earth. I love her truly and completely, more than I ever thought I could love anyone. She is truly my perfect partner. But—do I ever look at other women from a sexual perspective? Of course. I can't help it. It just happens. To turn that urge off would be like trying to turn off the sun. So if a man looks admiringly at another woman, it does not mean that he is unfaithful or that he doesn't love his partner. Remember—for a man, love and sex are totally different concepts.

Here is what happens in a typical male-female relationship. Man and woman start dating and eventually get around to having sex. It is sex in it purest form—physical pleasure. There is no love element at this point of the relationship. We have sex because it feels good—hopefully, anyway. Men do it because it not only feels good physically but also because that caveman part likes to conquer. It feeds our often fragile male egos. My guess is that women do it in part for the physical pleasure and in part because they know they have to in order to continue in the relationship and in part to lure the man to be attracted to them. Generally, most women are monogamous by nature and most men are not. My own experience has taught me that women tend to act one way before love and/or marriage and in a different way after. In other words, women will go all out to be alluring and sexy and fawn all over some guy until he says "I do". After he is hers, most women do not seem to feel the need to continue that pre-marital game. Now it is, "Hey, you, take out the garbage." This is a gross generalization, and may be slightly exaggerated. But only slightly. The point here is that before love and/or marriage, sex is sex. At some point, for women, sex becomes love. It is an expression of caring, tenderness, affection, and trust. It is not so much about physical pleasure any more. In some cases, it becomes about making babies, and sometimes, after the babies, it just becomes a chore and a bore.

A big issue in most marriages and long-term relationships is the difference between making love and having sex. When sex turns to love, women seem to be only interested in making love. That is the caring and tender act of mutual satisfaction and support and trust. Making love is a wonderful thing for both men and women, and men need to take the time and spend the effort to give their partners pleasure. A man should make his partner the center of his lovemaking and focus on meeting her needs. He should talk about what works and doesn't work for her. Conversely, women should make the same effort for their husbands. Sometimes maybe it should be her turn and sometimes his turn. If both parties make a commitment to focusing on satisfying their partner instead of focusing on their own desires, lovemaking can be wonderful for both. It is true that giving can be more rewarding than receiving.

There is a problem in all this bliss, though. Once a woman graduates from having sex to making love, the interest in sex is usually gone. Some sort of transition seems to occur, and after it occurs, there is no turning back. But men never lose interest in having sex. Making love is fine sometimes, maybe even most times, but once in awhile, a man just wants to have sex. I suspect that virtually every man will understand the difference between making love and having sex. I fear that few women will understand the distinction. I will try to explain. Sex is more of an attitude. It is more of a wild, unabashed coupling. The primary focus of sex is pure physical pleasure. It is maybe different from what a couple traditionally does in terms of technique and location. It is *yeah, baby, yahoo, and giddy-up*. It is something new. It is the fantasy you have always had but have been afraid to tell anyone. It is more raunchy and raw. And the truth is that men need and want this sometimes.

Why do so many couples have sexual and intimacy problems? It is because their expectations are different. They may even talk about the issue, but most times they are not talking the same language. Why do so many men in committed relationships masturbate, thrive on porn, or fool around with other women? Why is porn, both soft and hard, a multi-billion dollar business throughout the world? Is it because the subscribers do not love their partners? In some cases, maybe yes, but in most cases the men involved love their partners very deeply. The problem is that they are sexually frustrated. In some cases, where a woman openly disdains both making love and having sex, the male reactions described above are understandable. But what about the situation where the female partner says, "I don't understand! We make love on a consistent basis." Well—she just described the problem. They may in fact make love all the time. But the question every woman should ask herself is this: "When is the last time I had sex with my partner?" Making love is generally enough for a woman, but it is not generally enough for a man. To stay satisfied, once in awhile a man needs to have sex! And if he can have sex with his partner, then he will generally be a very happy man and not feel the need to masturbate, thrive on porn, or fool around with other women. He will still look and imagine but it will be far more fleeting and a lot less tempting.

What if the woman does not feel the urge, desire, or interest in having sex? That is certainly a personal choice. And that is something couples will have to work out the best they can. Some men can accept a life with no sex. Some men can even accept a life with no lovemaking. Some men can live with no sex as long as they can have their porn or other outlets. Some men can only live with that if they are getting sex on the side. And some men will look to dump their partner for someone else who does satisfy their needs. In the latter category is the stereotypical older man dumping his long-term wife for a younger woman. Odds are that in almost every case like this, the lack of lovemaking and/or the lack of sex was a significant motivating factor for the split. The truth is that men generally will always be interested in having sex and will for the most part abide making love. That caveman part, that part of the brain that never progressed past sixteen years of age, seems to stay with a man pretty much for as long as he lives. Why do you think drugs like Viagra are so popular? Viagra, in many cases, is more of a tonic to fight boredom in the bedroom than it is to address some physiological condition. Consider this: Catherine Zeta-Jones is universally recognized as one of the most physically beautiful women in the world. That should make Michael Douglas one of the happiest and most satisfied men in the world. Right? But if all the Douglases do year after year is make love, it is pretty much guaranteed that Michael Douglas will get bored and be sexually unsatisfied. Even making love to Catherine Zeta-Jones will not be enough to overcome his need for sex once in awhile. The point here is that sexual attractiveness is not so much about looks, weight, clothes, or a lot of other things that women get hung up on. Those kinds of things can be factors, but what is really most important is attitude. Most men would prefer an average looking woman with a great attitude towards sex and lovemaking than a goddess who is a cold fish.

Look at it this way. As a woman, how does it make you feel when your partner says you are the most beautiful woman in the world? Or that you made the best dinner he has ever had? Or when he willingly goes to see a chick-flick movie that you really want to see? Or he is nice to your mother whom he has never really liked that much? All these sorts of things are what? They are expressions of love. As a man, I like to do these sorts of things because it lets my wife know how much I love and appreciate her. Well, sex is also an expression of love. And so is making love. So even if the idea of wild, unabashed sex is not a big turn-on to you, you might consider it as a gift to your partner. Trust me—it will be a gift well remembered and more appreciated than you will ever know. It will also be like buying a good stock—it will pay dividends. When men feel satisfied and loved, they tend to be more thoughtful and loving in return.

The truth is that most relationships are governed by the actions of women. Men are more reactionary than initiatory. If the woman is in a good mood, the man probably will be. If the woman is loving, then most men will be loving in response. It may not be a fair distribution of responsibility. In fact, let's agree—it is not fair to women! But the reality is that a woman's attitude and actions set the course for most relationships and the men just climb on board and react. As a woman, you may not like things that way, but you would be a fool to not recognize the reality.

Chapter 3

The Truth about War

In my lifetime, my country has been involved in a number of wars. We are kind of like good old Lucas McCain of the old *Rifleman* TV series. He was a peace loving man who killed at least one or two people a show. Heck, after Lucas was done dispensing peace in the New Mexico Territory, there shouldn't have been a living soul left! So like Lucas Mc Cain, if we are such a peace loving nation, why do we always seem to be at war?

I was also a history major in college and have always been somewhat fascinated as to why somewhat normal, rational human beings are willing to slaughter other somewhat normal, rational human beings. Am I wrong here, or do most human beings want the same things, to wit, food, clothing, shelter, education, religious freedom, opportunities to live, work, and raise a family in peace, and freedom to make choices in all of the preceding? If everyone wants the same things in life, why do we kill each other?

Typically, wars are justified for a whole lot of different reasons. The most common justification in history is that some leader convinces his followers that their god has demanded that they wipe out all those who worship a different god. This is a curious justification since all religions preach essentially the same things. The terms and names and ceremonies are different but the basic fundamental teachings are very, very similar: be a good person, don't sin, treat each other with kindness and respect, don't violate other's rights, and praise your god. It seems especially hypocritical for Christians to justify war based upon religion since war goes against everything that Jesus Christ preached!

What have been some of the other justifications? To bring democracy to oppressed people. To destroy weapons of mass destruction. To end tyranny. To free slaves. To obtain independence. All good reasons, and all may have some degree of truth. But the real truth is that wars are started for one reason and one reason only—power and control. Someone wants to exercise power and control over someone else or someone wants to prevent a third party from exercising power and control over someone else. Every war ever fought was really about power and control. All the other justifications are merely excuses to rally the people to the cause or to justify actions taken.

The American Revolution was a battle for freedom from tyranny. That sounds so good. But what does it really mean? It means that the rich and powerful landowners in the colonies wanted to control their own destiny; they did not like the thought of the rich and powerful landowners in England controlling them. When England sought to exercise more and more control, and even took away some of the powers the colonists had traditionally exercised, war became inevitable. The American Revolution was really about who was going to control the economic (and hence political) future of the North American continent. Remember that there was a big push to invade Canada and make it part of the United States. If the Continental Army had been stronger and not so battered after seven or eight years of war, there would not be a Canada today. To the leaders of the time, the war was not for freedom's sake itself, it was for wresting economic and political control of the new colonies away from England and for themselves. And why did England resist?

Because it did not want these colonial interlopers taking power and control (meaning money and wealth) away from the crown. It wasn't just King George who had an issue with the colonies. It was the powerful English lords and merchants. Do you think there ever would have been a war if the colonists hadn't grown cash crops and provided other natural resources needed by England? What if the English court had granted more power and control to the colonists, especially those who controlled the economy? It is almost a certainty that if King George had given the American lords the same rights as the British lords, there would never have been a revolution.

The American Civil War was also about power and control. It is not that some well-meaning people did not care about slavery. But give me a break! Do you realize that probably the majority of northerners supported slavery, or were at least casually indifferent to it? The free blacks or escaped slaves who lived in the north suffered as much discrimination or more than many of those in the south. It is nice to think of noble people doing battle and sacrificing their lives solely to free an oppressed people. Truth—nice concept but not reality. So what was the Civil War really about? You guessed it—power and control. In the mid-1800s, the northern tier states were the industrial centers of the young country. The south was the agricultural center. The south politely shipped the raw goods up north to be manufactured and sold throughout the country. That worked great for the north because they made the most money and were able to control the economics and commerce of the country. At that time, remember, the country was pretty much limited to lands east of the Mississippi River. What changed all of that was the advent of the railroad and the explorations and discoveries in the west. All of a sudden there were vast new markets. The south decided that it did not want to be totally beholden to the north; it wanted to be able to ship goods directly out west to take advantage of the new markets. There was a long fight in Congress about building a transcontinental railroad and who would control it. There were proposals for a southern line, a northern line, and even a middle line. Because the north had more population and controlled the Congress, the southerners' attempt to have a westward-bound railroad line of their own was defeated. That was what led to the secession. The south wanted power and control over its agricultural goods. The north did not want to relinquish power and control over those goods and the wealth involved in manufacturing and controlling the new markets. Simply put, this war was inevitable when the Congress would not allow the south to market its own goods. The fact that the southern agrarian economy was slave dependent was just a coincidence. If slavery had not been part of the southern economy, the war would have happened just the same.

Even World Wars I and II are good examples. In both of those wars, the United States got involved well after the wars had started. In both cases, our concern was preventing others from exercising power and control over conquered lands. In WWI, we eventually decided, after considerable debate, by the way, that it was not in our best interests to let Germany control Europe. In WWII, with prompting by Japan, we once again eventually decided that it was not in our best interests to let Germany control Europe and Japan control Asia. But remember that the war in Europe and Asia had been going on for almost three years before we entered the fray. This was not a case of responding to the calls of allies. It was a case of weighing whether or not it mattered to us that two other countries would have power and control over most of the civilized world. Ultimately, economically, if for no other reason, it made sense to us not to allow Germany and Japan to exercise that kind of power and control. Would we have entered the war without Pearl Harbor? No question the answer is yes. Roosevelt was looking for any excuse to sell it to the American people. You know the old maxim, "Where there is a will, there is a way." Recall the infamous Gulf of Tonkin incident wherein President Lyndon Johnson used the North Vietnamese "attack" as justification for us to get really involved in Vietnam.

And Vietnam? Power and control over the economics of that area of the world was the issue. We did not want Russia or China to dominate and have power and control over the region. We felt we needed an economic and military presence in the area. The fight for freedom of the South Vietnamese was a ruse, plain and simple. The region was deemed too valuable strategically to let our rivals have power and control there. The irony is that neither China nor Russia would ever have been able to control the Vietnamese. Our biggest sin here was being too ignorant to know or appreciate the history of the region. Every life lost here, on both sides, was wasted. We fought this war based on the totally faulty premise that, if we let the Vietnamese decide their own political destiny, they would end up being dominated and controlled by either the Russians or the Chinese. The hot-button label used to justify the war was that we did not want the "communists" to control Vietnam. Yet a study of the region's history would have shown that the Vietnamese people had been fighting wars on and off for centuries to maintain their independence from China, France, and anyone else who tried to control them. They might have been communist in name but they would not have been anyone's puppet. As history has proven, since the North Vietnamese prevailed, the country today is communist in name but is fiercely independent and poses no threat, strategic or otherwise, to the United States. The bigger tragedy is that we still do not seem to have learned the lesson that cost fifty thousand American lives and hundreds of thousands wounded. We continue to wage war based on faulty premises without having seemingly learned anything from our mistakes.

And Iraq? Well, it obviously was not about weapons of mass destruction. It would be pretty hypocritical if it had been, since North Korea, Iran, Pakistan, India, and others have such weapons and we don't seem to be too excited about it—at least not to the point of invading these countries. It certainly is not about bringing democracy to oppressed people. Once again, if that was our real reason, are we going to invade Saudi Arabia? China? Any one of a number of dictatorships in South and Central America? Historically, we tend to support dictators as long as they pay lip service to us. The real reasons for the Iraq war are still unclear but time will shed more light and better conclusions may be drawn. But since wars are always about power and control, it is a good guess that our government feared that specific terrorists or certain terrorist groups might be exercising too much power and control in Iraq. Iraq had the military know-how, capacity, and willingness to arm and equip terrorists like no one before it. There was the fear, and maybe rightly so, that Iraq could become a true terrorist state that would pose a direct threat to the United States. So it wasn't so much that we wanted to exercise power and control in Iraq, it was that we did not want to let terrorists have that opportunity. Call it a preemptive self-defense move. If this theory is accurate, look for some action against Iran sometime in the future. Perhaps it was also that we wanted to exercise more power and control over the Iraqi oil fields, or maybe the truth is some combination of these two theories. As I said, time will let us be a better judge of the why behind the war.

The Iraq war is a classic example of failing to learn from our past mistakes. We learned, or should have learned, in the Vietnam War that trying to be a "police force" in a country torn by civil war was a no-win situation for us. This is especially true in a country where we are truly foreigners with no common language, religion, or history. Had we left after deposing Saddam Hussein, there would have been a civil war in Iraq. After all, we created a power vacuum and with the factions in that country, it should have been obvious there was going to be a fight to fill that void. However, once we finally leave Iraq, they will have their civil war anyway. All our presence has done is to delay the inevitable. And what about all those Americans who died or were wounded? What was it for? Just as in Vietnam, it may all have been for nothing. That is not to say that we should not honor those soldiers who fought and died or were wounded. As soldiers, they answered the call of their government and should be honored for doing so. The soldier is merely a tool of war and never to blame for the folly of the government.

One last thing on war and history. What is history? Is it what actually happened? Or is it what was reported to have happened? The truth is that the winners write the history. What you see or read or hear may bear little resemblance to what factually occurred. Isn't it interesting how only losers commit genocide? What would the history books say if we had sat out World War II and Germany now controlled all of Europe and Japan controlled all of Asia? Would Hitler be a villain? Would we have ever heard of the holocaust? Because historical truths are what some writer says they are, the perceptions and biases of the historical reporters become the actual history. We have no way to go back in time machines to view the actual events, so we rely on the accounts of others, and how accurate are those accounts? I have read newspaper accounts of events that I know for an absolute fact distort or misstate what actually occurred. Even firsthand accounts in letters or journals are full of biases or misperceptions. In my thirty-two-plus years of practicing criminal law, I have seen so many, many circumstances where honest witnesses describe the same event drastically differently— so much so you sometimes wonder if they are talking about the same event! We are all different and so our senses perceive things differently from everyone else's. Because our senses are unique and our life experiences are unique, no two people will ever perceive something exactly the same. So what is historical truth? The truth is that we will never know real historical truth. The best we can do is to understand that we are relying on other people's perceptions. We need to understand that everyone has biases and we should factor those in when deciding how much credibility we are going to give to any information.

The point here is that you should go ahead and read and listen, but be critical of what you perceive from others. When you hear a politician trying to justify a war, listen with your ears but listen with your brain, too, and think about issues of control and power. You may decide to support a particular war, but at least you should be doing so for the right reasons. Wars are never fought for only truly noble causes. There is always a seamy side. Sometimes that seamy side may be justified from a self-defense point of view, or maybe you just want to dominate someone else and take what they have. Wouldn't that be a treat? A leader tells his people that they are going to war because he wants what their neighbor has and he believes that his army can kick the crap out of their army! That would be *true* history, but it is a sure thing that you will never read that quote in the history books!

Chapter 4

The Truth about Education

In my sixty-plus years, so much has changed in the world about how we lead our day-to-day lives. Technology has caused the largest change. Today we have instant communication in multiple forms, be it cell phones, pagers, fax machines, instant messages, camera phones, etc. As I think back on my life experience, hardly anything is the same now as it was when I was a child, except for our approach to education. When my kids were in school, it was like a blast from the past as far as subject matters, report requirements, and the general approach to education. The content of the classes was more sophisticated and complicated, but the same basic educational philosophy still existed. If you think about it, our approach to education really hasn't changed much over the last few hundred years. Oh, there are nuances of change here and there but we still teach math, science, history, and reading courses as standard fare. The changes, if any, are only in how we teach the same subjects we have always taught. Throw in a language, art, or music course, and physical education, and a child's course schedule today looks much like the course schedule of one hundred years ago. Frankly, no one seems to question this approach or ever seems to want to update our thinking about education. Are we really teaching kids what they need to know? Did someone discover the magic formula hundreds of years ago and therefore there is no need to analyze what we teach? Are our kids so well educated that we are totally satisfied with the education system? Unless you have just returned from a galaxy far, far away, it is hard to believe that anyone would think that our education system is doing a great job.

Now, I am not professing to be an expert in the area of education. I am also not professing to have all the answers. But isn't it about time that we at least discuss and think about modernizing our education system? Ford doesn't build cars the same way it did one hundred years ago. Clothing isn't manufactured the same way it was in the early 1900s. The building codes for houses and commercial building are constantly being updated. It would actually be illegal to build a house today the same way one would have a hundred years ago. What I am suggesting is that we need to evaluate whether we need to update the building code for what we teach our children.

What is the purpose of education? Hopefully, it is more than to provide publicly funded baby-sitting, although, in some cases, it appears that is pretty much what it has come down to. Since the dawn of mankind, education has served one primary purpose—to enable children to become functional adults in the society of the time. At one point in time, the most important things children needed to learn included how to grow crops, track an animal, shoot an arrow, and prepare hides, if they were going to become contributing and functioning adults. As times have changed, what is needed to be a functional member of society has also changed. Is our education system doing the best it can to prepare our kids to be contributing and functional adults in today's society? Or are we using the approach we have always used because—well, we have always used it?

The first thing that needs to be determined is what makes a successful, functioning adult in today's society? Certainly, the basics of being able to read and write and do basic math still exist and will continue to exist. There is nothing wrong with a well-rounded education that includes history, art, music, and knowledge of the geo-political world as it exists today, but it is hard to imagine in our modern world anyone being able to thrive without significant computer skills. By the time they graduate from high school, all children should know computers and the latest software inside and out. Some form of computer education should be given every single year from grade one to grade twelve. And what about everyday life skills? How about a class or series of classes that teach mundane but necessary skills like how to open and maintain a bank account; how to buy a house; how to shop for a loan; how to buy a car; how to do basic household repairs; how to prepare a résumé; how to interview for a job; basics about leases and landlord-tenant laws; what you need to know about credit? And even more importantly, how about some education about child care and development? How about some training about interpersonal relationships? How about a class on teenage problems and issues? How about a class on teenage development? The truth is that the most important things we need to know to live a happy and productive life we learn from observing our parents (and that might be okay *if* the parents have any clue about what they are doing), other families, or on our own. The problem with this approach is that it is a crap shoot when it comes to quality. The reality is that good *and* bad habits tend to get passed on from one generation to the other.

In my experience and that of my children, schools tend to spend way too much time on make-work projects and useless knowledge. It is axiomatic that part of learning is learning how to learn. But let's get real. How much of the trigonometry I learned in high school do I either remember or ever use? NONE! And although I recall that the Battle of Hastings took place in 1066, what good has that information ever done for me as an adult? NONE! Think of all the countless hours spent doing stupid, make-work projects. Or think of all the Civil War maps made showing the various battles. How about having to memorize and recite the prologue to *The Canterbury Tales* in Middle English? And the point was? The point here is that there is plenty of time in the current curriculum to incorporate meaningful and useful education as well as the traditional academic pap that we have been fed. Teaching children about history shouldn't require that they memorize a bunch of useless dates. A better approach is to teach about the lessons of history without sweating all of the minute details. The same with math—teach the basics, but there is absolutely no need to get in to the finer points of complex calculations. No one ever remembers that stuff and everyone has computers to do the calculations anyway. The truth of the matter is that ninety-nine percent of adults don't need to know much more than basic addition, subtraction, multiplication, and division. In my life, all the math I ever really needed to know I learned by fourth grade. In social studies, do kids really need to memorize the capital of every country? Why? If you need to know the capital of Botswana, it is more important to know how to find the answer than to know the answer itself. Part of the problem with our current educational approach is that we seem to get lost in the details and have forgotten or ignored the purpose of teaching a particular subject matter. We focus so much on *what* we are teaching we end up ignoring the more important question of *why*. The first question that should be asked in teaching any subject is why? Then the teaching can be tailored to reach the objective. And if the kids understand the why, they will be more receptive to the learning process. Our approach of requiring encyclopedic knowledge of facts without any context makes little lasting impression on most kids. And more importantly, our current system fails to teach most of the things that children will really need to know to be able to function as competent adults in today's society. I am not suggesting that everyone should agree with my views. But it is clearly about time to reevaluate our educational system—what we teach, why we teach it, how we teach it, and what else should we be teaching. This process should involve parents, educators, students, business leaders, and relevant professionals, like child development specialists. When is the last time this country took a comprehensive, analytical, and all-inclusive look at its educational system? Unfortunately, the answer is never.

Chapter 5

The Truth about Living in a "Democracy"

The title of this section is wrong, of course. We do not live in a democracy. We live in a republic. In a true democracy, all the people have the opportunity to participate in all governmental decisions. In a republic, the people delegate their authority over governmental affairs to elected representatives. By and large, we, as voters, do not make the laws, but rather choose those who make the laws. The notable exception to this, as frequently seen in California, is legislation by ballot proposition. That is true democracy in action.

Our form of democracy is pretty well acknowledged as one of the most inefficient forms of government. That is the price of freedom—inefficiency. The form of government with the least individual freedom is a one-person dictatorship. That is also the most efficient form of government. A truly benevolent dictatorship would probably be the "best" form of government. The problem is obvious—benevolent to whom? A few select people, or the majority? History has repeatedly shown us that "power corrupts and absolute power corrupts absolutely." I often think that the world would be a better place if I were anointed czar over the planet, but the truth is that no human being can wield that much power without being adversely effected and corrupted. So—let's stick with our so-called democracy.

With such a noble idea, how come so many people are frustrated by our government? Why doesn't it work better? Why are so many of our own people distrustful of our elected representatives at the local, state, and national level?

First, some dissatisfaction is inevitable. There are too many people in this country with too many divergent views about too many issues for everyone to ever be completely satisfied. The basic premise of our government is that the majority rules. Of course, that means for virtually every issue, someone is going to be unhappy with the decision. Unfortunately, we seem to have become a society where doing what is best for the whole no longer matters. It has come down to "what is best for me and to hell with everyone else." With that attitude so prevalent, it is not hard to understand why there is so much dissatisfaction. In my thirty-two-plus years in government, I also noticed an interesting phenomenon—the "what have you done for me lately" syndrome. It seemed like no matter how well you performed a public service for someone or for how long, the one time that you made a decision the person didn't like, you were all of a sudden a worthless *****. This reaction is really just an example of the "do what is right for me and the hell with everyone else" mind-set that so many people have these days. The point of all of this is that dissatisfaction with government, in part, may stem from our own selfish view of things. Just because things weren't decided our way doesn't necessarily mean that government officials are stupid, corrupt, or worthless. It also doesn't necessarily mean that the government isn't working properly. In fact, if you represent the minority view on an issue, it may mean that the government did exactly what is was designed to do in siding with the majority.

All that being said, a lot of problems in government are institutional. In my many years of government service, due to the nature of my assignments, I had the opportunity to deal with a *lot* of public officials at all levels. My first lesson in how government really works occurred when I had graduated from law school. I was awaiting my orders from the Air Force on when and where to report for duty. At some time considerably prior to graduating from law school, I had filled out a "dream sheet" indicating the bases I would prefer and what Air Force command I would prefer. I requested a number of bases—all were either on the west coast or east coast. And I requested any Air Force command but specifically *not* SAC (Strategic Air Command). You guessed it—I was assigned to SAC HQ in Omaha, Nebraska! My schooling in how government really works had begun!

If I had the power to change or modify our government for the better, I would address the following areas. The first applies specifically to legislatures. What is the purpose of any legislature? The answer—to pass laws. For over two hundred years now, we have had local, state, and national legislatures passing more and more laws. We are by far and away the most regulated society in history. Has that made life better? Are we safer now than we were two hundred years ago? The truth is that in some ways we may be better and in some ways we may be worse. The problem is that our regulatory systems and our laws are so complex that the average person can't begin to fathom what is and is not allowed under all our rules and regulations. Most of us just use common sense, and for the most part that works. It is likely that most of us violate some law or another on a regular basis and have no idea we are doing so. But what does a newly elected legislator want to do when he or she takes office? Pass some more laws! That is what legislators prides themselves on—making new (and thus more) laws. How about mandating that for every new law that is enacted, each legislature has to repeal a law? In reality, each legislature should spend the time necessary to review all the various laws and update the codes and repeal all the unnecessary junk that is in there. Maybe even have a session or two (or more) where there is a moratorium on passing any new laws, using the time to do something more useful like modernizing, updating, and simplifying the volumes, volumes, and volumes of laws that we already have. I once read an article that claimed that ninety percent of the laws passed in California were special interest legislation. I don't know if that is true but even if it is only half true—enough!

So you decide that you want to run for office and serve your community, state, or federal government. In my experience, many people who run for office the first time do so with noble ideals of making things better. But the political bug must bite people after they get sworn in, because for the vast majority of elected or appointed officials, the most important item on the agenda from that point on is to get reelected or reappointed. The rationalization goes something like this—*I am doing such a wonderful job that I need to do whatever it takes to stay in office so I can continue to do wonderful things.* Most political officials, at some point in their careers, become legends in their own minds. So now that you are convinced that the people cannot possibly get by without you in office, what do you need to do to stay in office? The usual answer is to raise money, and lots of it. How do you do that? The typical, the most effective, and the most lucrative way is to support and or sponsor special interest legislation that benefits the few, often at the expense of the majority. Special interest groups tend to raise a lot of money and they are usually very clever and sophisticated at doling that money out to get what they want. If you oppose a particular group or groups, well, you can bet that your opponent in the next election will be getting the money that could have gone to you. In defense of public officials, in order to compete in the election system we have nowadays, you are almost forced to sell your soul. Unless you are independently wealthy, you can't win elections without having to raise money, and the lion's share of money in political contributions comes from special interest groups. Even if you are self funded, if there are enough special interest groups opposed to you, they have an uncanny ability through smear campaigns to unduly influence an election.

As a side note, most people don't realize that there is no "truth in advertising" law that covers political speech. "Political speech" is and has been vigorously protected by the Supreme Court. That is a good thing, on one hand. The ability to speak freely is a cornerstone of our republic. The unfortunate result, however, is that people running for office or people backing those or opposing those running for office, can pretty much lie their asses off with no legal consequences whatsoever. It is up to us, the electorate, to discern the truth. Right! Who has the time or resources to do that?

There does not appear to be a perfect solution to dealing with the above stated issues. Two ideas, however, merit some consideration. The first is public financing of campaigns. This is certainly not a novel idea of mine, but one that has been proposed by a number of people for a long time. The advantage of public financing is that it takes special interest money out of the equation, at least to some extent. Everyone is on an equal footing, moneywise. Candidates would be prohibited from taking or spending any money on a campaign that comes from any source other than the public financing fund. If politicians didn't have to worry so much about raising money all the time, maybe they could or would focus more on you and me and the issues of the day. This is not a perfect solution. Special interest groups could still independently support or oppose a candidate. But at least that would be apparent, rather than happening surreptitiously by means of campaign contributions.

The second idea is to have term limits for all elected and or appointed offices. Again, this is hardly a novel idea. The argument against term limits is that those elected are not given the chance to develop the expertise they need to effectively run the government. To some extent, this makes sense. The solution, therefore, is to extend the terms of office. For example, a United States Senate seat could be held for eight or ten years. A House seat could be held for six years. A Presidential term could be for six years. The length of terms would have to be debated, but the idea has some merit. If no one could ever run for reelection, those elected would be motivated to do the job during their one term in office. Too many officials make decisions, not based upon what is best for their constituency, but based on what they think will best help them get reelected. That is just the stone cold truth.

There is a fallacy to the "experience" argument, also. The truth is that most governments are run not by the elected officials but by the career bureaucrats or staffers. The term bureaucrat has come to have a bad connotation (see my discussions about labels) but there are many very dedicated, very qualified, and very capable public servants who work long hours for less then they could make in private industry and without whom the government simply could not run. It's like the military—most vets will tell you that the service is really run by the sergeants, not the generals. When I was in the Air Force, if I really wanted something done, I contacted the sergeant in charge of a particular unit, not the commander. Even a newly elected official can tap into a vast reservoir of experience around him or her. It should be the elected official's job to be the leader, to set goals and priorities, to inspire, and to enable his or her staff to accomplish certain goals. The official doesn't need to be, and probably shouldn't be, the nuts and bolts person. Therefore, experience may be seriously overrated.

The last area of real concern is the partisanship that threatens to destroy our government. No matter what side of the political fence you are on, it should be patently obvious to anyone who remotely pays attention to government what is going on locally and in Washington, D.C. We have, for all intents and purposes, only two political parties in this country. The problem with only having two parties is that when one party can gain control of the government, it seeks to do its will and the other party be damned. Both Republicans and Democrats are equally guilty. In many countries there are multiple political parties and in order to exercise control (i.e., create a majority), parties have to align with one another. That requires compromise. In our system, compromise seems to be a dirty word, only used when absolutely necessary. How many times have you heard about a situation where a Democrat/Republican proposes something that sounds pretty good, but no matter how good it sounds the other party immediately dismisses the idea or attacks it? When the other party is in power they propose almost the identical idea and the opposing party now assails it. It's absurd! Yet this scenario seems to go on all the time. When someone is elected to office, that person is supposed to represent not only those who voted for him/her, but *all* the people of that jurisdiction. The official is supposed to represent citizens, not the bosses of a political party (who may live in a totally different part of the country), but it seems more and more that the ultra left wing or right wing ideologues who get elected to run the political parties are really the ones calling the shots. These people control our representatives and yet we never get to choose them in a real election. We rarely even know who they are, but they wield enormous power! Remember the elected official's first mantra—get reelected. What if you stand up to your party boss and vote your conscience or what you think is best for your constituency as opposed to the "party line?" You may not get the party support at the next election. The bosses will probably run someone against you in the party primary. Again, much like special interest groups (and what is a political party but a special interest group?), well-meaning public officials sometimes have little or no choice but to go along with party dictates even if they personally disagree or even if it is not in the best interests of their constituency. So who do *our* elected officials represent, you and me, or some party boss?

Once someone is elected, he or she should be a *United States* Senator, not a Republican or Democratic senator. The same with the House and the same with all officials elected to partisan offices. How about this for a change in Congress and the state legislatures—

do the seating by seniority, or alphabetically, but not by political party! It is counterproductive to emphasize the party divisions. It shouldn't be about political parties once you are elected! It *should* be about what is best for the greatest number of people. Once again, strict term limits and public financing would severely diminish the control and power wielded by the political party power brokers.

Obviously, one or more Constitutional amendments would be necessary to make some of the changes proposed, at least on the federal level. Is that likely to happen? Yeah—when pigs fly! There is no way that those in power are going to agree to modify the system such that it will effectively limit their influence and power. The only way any changes will ever be made is for the general public to demand it—loudly and over and over. Even then it would probably take a national effort to elect people who would support the changes.

The most frustrating thing about government is when you see national polls indicating strong support for or opposition to a particular issue, and yet Congress does nothing, or worse, Congress ends up acting contrary to the public will. I'm not sure it would ever be feasible, but it would certainly be interesting if we had a national referendum where the people could enact laws or effectuate changes in government. Now, *that* would be true democracy!

Chapter 6

The Truth about Religion

Throughout history, the discussion about religion has always been a real hot-button issue. When you discuss something tangible, something that you can see, touch, hear, feel, or smell, most of the obvious traits are usually non-debatable. In other words, there is usually some amount of agreement and disagreements are usually limited to subtleties. I mean, a six-foot tall piece of granite is just that. But in the spiritual world, since virtually everything is a matter of belief or faith with little or no tangible evidence of the "truth," almost everything is open to debate and disagreement. How is anyone to know for an absolute certainty what "truth" is when it comes to spiritual matters? The truth is that we can't. It is all a matter of conjecture, faith, and personal belief.

Whatever one chooses to call it, religion, faith, spirituality, etc., there is no question that "it" has been a true blessing for billions of people who have walked on the earth. Faith in God or godlike entities has helped people get through and cope with every imaginable type of crisis. Faith has inspired genius, cured the sick, provided hope when all looked to be lost, sparked kindness, love, and charity, and been the genesis of untold number of other good acts and deeds.

Ironically, it really hasn't mattered which god or gods were being worshipped. From the gods of the pantheon, to various sun gods, to animals, to Jehovah, to Jesus, to Allah, to literally thousands of other objects or entities being worshipped, all have inspired true blessings. The mind and spirit of the worshipper seems to be more important than the actual god or spirit being worshipped. Unfortunately, the converse is also true. Many an evil has been inspired by the exact same gods or spirits. Over our history as a species, think of all the poor souls who have been killed, maimed, and tortured in the name of some god. Again, it seems to be the frame of mind of the individual worshipper that determines whether the message received results in loving acts or what most people would typically call evil acts. Good and evil are, after all, relative terms. The point here is that we focus too much on the source of spirituality and not nearly enough on us, the receivers. For example, in western society today, Allah probably has a bad name because of the association of Allah with what we call terrorists. Yet the belief in Allah has also inspired millions of his followers to live noble, peace-loving, positive and productive lives. So arguing, and fighting, and killing each other over the issue about what god is the true god is absurd. It doesn't matter! What is more important—the source of the message, or the result? Imagine you had a neighbor who was kind, thoughtful, generous, considerate, loving, and selfless towards you and your family. On the other side, you had a neighbor who was rude, loud, obnoxious, dirty, and a mean drunk. Which one would you prefer? Which one would you like all the rest of your neighbors to be like? Which one would you like the rest of your fellow citizens to be like? Would it change your opinion if the first neighbor worshipped trees and the second neighbor worshipped and regularly attended the local (pick your religion) church? This should be a no-brainer. Why should you or I care what inspires someone to act in a "blessed way?" It should be the actions that count, not the particular motivation.

As stated previously, every human being that has ever walked or crawled on the face of the earth is unique. None of us are or ever have been or ever will be *exactly* alike. So isn't it logical that it might take different things to motivate different people? Shouldn't we judge people by their actions as opposed to their beliefs? If the actions are productive and positive (i.e., blessed), what difference does it make what belief system motivated those actions? Similarly, if someone acts negatively and destructively, is that then okay because their belief system is the same as ours? Let's put it this way; would you rather live in a world of almost seven billion people where every person had his or her own unique "god" but everyone treated everyone else with love, consideration, and kindness, or in a world where everyone believed in the exact same "god" but treated each other with contempt, distrust, and dishonesty? Why does my motivation to be a good person have to be the same as yours? Or why does yours have to be the same as mine?

This brings us to organized religion. Organized religion, by its very nature, tends to be exclusionary, valuing the process over the result. Why is every religion exclusionary? Because each religion presumes and operates under the premise that it knows the one and only path to "God." Each religion is predicated on the basis that its followers, if true to its particular doctrines and rituals, will ultimately find God/heaven/nirvana/etc. The opposite is also true—non-believers will not find God, etc. In other words, each religion believes and preaches that its "way" is the one and only true way and that every other way is wrong. The process of getting to God becomes more important than the result of believing in that system. As long as you believe in and follow a certain process, no matter what you actually do or how you actually act, you will be on the path to God. Does that really make sense to anyone? Why can't there be multiple paths to God? Don't you think that God, whoever and whatever he, she, or it is, would rather have us treat each other with compassion, respect, civility, kindness, and love than all agree on a certain ritualistic system but not treat each other with compassion, respect, civility, kindness, and love? Are we not truly creatures of God? And on an every day level don't we judge each other by how we act? It is in our nature to be that way. Then why wouldn't God care more about what we do and how we act than the belief system that motivates us? There is an old expression—actions speak louder than words. Maybe there should be a new expression—actions are more important than motivations. Or—actions are more important than beliefs. Imagine a world in which we valued each other on how we behaved, a world where we were grateful for each and every person that behaved in a "blessed" way and could honor whatever it took to inspire that conduct in that person. If we could all do that, would the world be better off than it is today? Something to think about, certainly.

Then, of course, there is the ugly aspect of organized religion. That is the desire to have power and control over others so that they will do your will. Not so much today, but historically, many religious leaders were more generals, kings, and dictators than true followers of any faith. Karl Marx once said that religion was the opiate of the masses. What he meant was that religion was used to control people and pacify them so that they would not revolt against their leaders. The intertwining of organized religion and government was commonplace. The abuses involved in this incestuous relationship were clearly a main motivating factor in our founding fathers mandating a separation between church and state. It wasn't that they didn't want God in our schools, businesses, or government institutions (as claimed by some), it was they didn't want church leaders involved in dictating government policy or in steering us towards a specific state-sponsored religion. Note the distinction—the intent of our founding fathers was *never* to take God out of public institutions! In fact, quite to the contrary, it was assumed that God was crucial to our nation's well-being, hence the verbiage "In God We Trust" and "One Nation Under God." But the founding fathers saw a distinction between God and the leaders of the various organized religions. The idea of separation between organized religions (church) and the state was to control the influence of certain people, to wit, religious leaders, on matters of state. In other words, God was a welcome influence and guide but the founding fathers did not want any particular religion or its leaders to have undue influence on the government and hence the doctrine of separation of *church* and state. I reiterate—the separation was to be between church and state not God and state!

You need look no farther than certain countries in the Middle East to see how religion is used to control the masses today. It is a lot more about power and control to benefit those in charge than it is about true religious faith. It is literally the oldest trick in the book— convince people that God wants things done a certain way; a way that ends up really only benefiting a small group of those either seeking to obtain something they don't have or seeking to maintain something they already have—to wit, absolute power and control. It is a simple case of manipulation of the masses by the few for the benefit of the few. Surely you can think of any number of religious organizations, both currently and historically, that have become tremendously wealthy and powerful while many of their followers live in squalor and poverty. Why is it that so many religious "leaders" live in splendor while their faithful often live day to day and hand to mouth? The truth—because it is not about religion or faith; it is about power and control and the perks and benefits that come with such power and control. The point here is not that organized religion is necessarily bad but that religion can be used (and has been used) for personal gain and the amassing of power. In other words, it is not the institution itself that is potentially dangerous, but the misuse of the institution by some people that has created and can create human suffering and misery.

Once again, I am not suggesting that organized religion is bad. Various religious groups have done wonderful things for millions and millions of people, often at great personal sacrifice. But I do suggest that all religions and their respective followers would be better served if they respectfully acknowledged that there may be other paths to God. If we could honor all those who seek God and act in a blessed way, no matter the path chosen, wouldn't the world be a better place?

Chapter 7

The Truth about Illegal Drugs

In this area, the truth may be too much for most Americans to accept, but after spending four years as an Air Force JAG (legal officer) and over twenty-eight years as a deputy district attorney, I believe that I know something about the drug issues in America. Our historic approach to dealing with illegal drugs is to go after the dealers, wholesale suppliers, and growers or manufacturers. We have spent billions (maybe trillions) of dollars trying to eradicate the supply side of the equation. A recent article said that the United States spends forty billion dollars each year in trying to eradicate the illegal drug trade. The same article quotes a United Nations study saying that the worldwide illegal drug trade is valued at three hundred forty billion dollars a year. A 1985 study claimed that drug-related illness, death, and crime costs us nearly sixty-seven billion dollars annually. That figure would obviously be much higher today. Most of our prisons are filled with people caught up in the business side of the illegal drug trade. And how much progress have we made? How much effect have we had on foreign countries where they continue to grow and manufacture illegal drugs? Have we slowed that supply down at all? Yes, there have been arrests and labs have been shut down. Tons and tons of illegal drugs have been seized, as well as tons of cash and weapons. Some big drug bust makes for good TV, but what has been the overall effect of all of our efforts? Probably the best that can really be said is that we have made a number of criminals filthy rich. The truth is that illegal drugs are today and will continue to be a huge business enterprise. Shutting down one supplier only affords someone else the opportunity to take his place. Shutting down one manufacturer only means that someone else has more business. Our current Secretary of State, Hilary Clinton, was recently quoted decrying this country's "insatiable appetite" for illegal drugs. And that is where the real problem is and where the solution lies.

We first have to recognize that the illegal drug trade is a business, and it is a very lucrative business. Forget about the morality issues relating to drug usage. Those issues are really irrelevant. We don't need moralists to help solve our drug issues, we need economists. Economics 101 teaches us about supply and demand. Where you have a demand for a product or a service, there will *always* be someone to provide the supply. Supply does not create the demand, but demand will always create the supply! That is why prostitution has existed from the dawn of man and will continue to exist as long as there are men and women. We can prosecute drug dealers and manufacturers until the cows come home, and as long as the demand continues to exist, there will continue to be a never-ending supply. There is just too much money to be made to not meet the demand. So what to do? If we do not want to legalize drugs, there is only one other solution. That solution may seem draconian to some but the answer is obvious—change our focus. Instead of focusing most of our efforts on the supply side, redirect those efforts to dealing with the demand side. Let's face it, if there is no demand, there is nothing to supply and the illegal drug business dries up.

How do we deal effectively with the demand side of the equation? Many have advocated treatment programs to deal with users. In some cases this approach has had some positive results, but the truth is that treatment programs historically have had limited success. The recidivism rate in almost all programs is extraordinarily high. A certain segment of the drug-using culture simply doesn't want to stop using. For any program to be effective, the participant has to want to quit, and even then, success rates are very low. Here comes the hard truth—the only effective way to curtail significantly the demand for illegal drugs in this country is to make the penalty for use and possession far more severe. When my parents were visiting Singapore, the authorities were going to execute two Dutch teenagers who brought a small amount of marijuana into the country. I am not suggesting that drug users be executed, but the point is that if there is a national will to make certain kinds of conduct unacceptable at whatever cost it takes, then it can be done. For juveniles, we have to continue to emphasize counseling and treatment over incarceration, but for adults, how about making any first time drug offense a felony with a mandatory jail sentence of not less than one year? A second offense could warrant a mandatory prison sentence of some indeterminate length, say five to ten years. The length of the sentence could depend on the person's conduct in prison and willingness to *truly* participate in drug counseling and treatment. A third offense would result in a life sentence. This is admittedly a harsh remedy, but the truth is that nothing else has worked! If we ever want to really solve our illegal drug problems, and all the collateral consequences like robberies, burglaries, murders, assaults, etc, then we *must* take a different approach. We have proved over and over that attacking the supply side doesn't work. If we continue in that approach, all we will really accomplish is to pour money down the rat hole into the pockets of criminals. Since elimination of the demand results in the *de facto* elimination of the supply and suppliers, that is the only logical approach. Obviously, how we do that will be open to some very vigorous debate. Included in that debate would have to be a discussion about what drugs should be included in this system. Do we include all drugs that are now listed as being illegal or do we have a different system for something like marijuana?

Very few people I know, if any, haven't either used drugs themselves or had one or more of their kids use drugs. I certainly include myself in that number on both accounts, but a lot of the drug usage resulted from the lax attitude that seemed to be prevalent in society. There is no question that if we really dedicated ourselves to attacking the demand side of the problem, one component would have to be education at all levels. We would have to start in the schools as early as kindergarten, and we would have to stick to our guns. That means that there will be some straight A student, a good kid, who will find his or her life drastically altered because of one mistake in judgment, but the only way to convince all kids and adults that, as a society, we really mean illegal drug use is *not* acceptable is to be tough and consistent, with no exceptions. Yes— at times, some unfairness may result, but that should more than be balanced by the overall good for our society and country. I have read some estimates that, without illegal drug use, crime rates in this country would drop by as much as 50 to 75 percent! Think of the massive economic savings. Think of the peace of mind. Think of the health of our kids. The only question is do we have the guts and the fortitude to face the truth and do what is necessary to solve this national epidemic?

Chapter 8

The Truth about Our "Melting Pot"

I was originally going to title this section "The Truth about Race Relations," but after thinking about it for sometime, it appears that in today's society the differences in cultures are probably more significant to us than the differences in races. At least this appears to be true in America.

The basic underlying premise to this chapter is this: People, as a general rule, are more comfortable being around their own kind. I realize that it is not politically correct to say this. In many ways, this premise is the elephant in the room that no one wants to admit is actually there, but almost everyone secretly acknowledges. My daughter went to an affluent public high school where the student body was made up of several different ethnic groups. The parents of these kids were generally highly educated professionals of one sort or another. The test scores at this school were very high and almost all the kids were college bound. Yet whenever I visited the school during recess or other school breaks, the kids divided themselves into their various ethnic groups. There were exceptions, of course, but generally, without any coercion or outside pressure that I was aware of, the kids just sort of naturally grouped with other kids of their same ethnicity. I later talked to my daughter about my observations and she confirmed that what I had noticed was the way it was. From what I have read and seen at other schools and universities, this is not a unique phenomenon. I've observed similar conduct in the workplace, at social events, in neighborhoods, and throughout our society. Why? Sometimes what appear to be complicated questions really have simple answers. People, as a general rule, are more comfortable being around their own kind! That is just the plain, unvarnished truth.

Is this phenomenon a bad thing? It certainly doesn't have to be. Going back to my daughter's high school—were the various ethnic groups going around and terrorizing the other groups? No! The kids, when mixed together, like in class or on sports teams, all seemed to get along fine. There didn't seem to be any animosity among the groups. To function as a school, they could and did mix perfectly well, but when on their own time, they generally preferred the company of their own ethnic group.

To an extent, our American society today is similar. Ethnic groups still tend to congregate by neighborhood, social groups, and other means. If you drive through any major metropolitan or suburban area, it is not at all difficult to see specific areas dominated by a particular ethnic or racial group. Is this just a coincidence or happenstance? Of course not! So let's just admit the truth—it's really okay. People, much like the animal population, as a general rule, are more comfortable being around their own kind. And it's okay as long as we treat each other with respect and civility. Amazingly, for being as ethnically diverse as we are, we all seem to get along fairly well. We generally work and live together and make things work. There are exceptions, of course, and probably always will be. But the important thing to note is that racial incidents in this country are the *exception,* not the rule. The point here is that even though it is apparent that different ethnic and racial groups prefer to be around their own kind, we all still manage to work and live together and, by and large, treat each other with dignity and respect. We are a melting pot, and the differences in race and ethnicity, per se, do not seem to pose a big problem for us as a country.

All that being said, there does appear to be a significant problem, but it has more to do with differences in culture than differences in race or ethnicity. In my lifetime of sixty years, one of the biggest changes I have noticed is the attitude of those immigrating to America. It used to be that people coming from some other country came here not only wanting a better life, but wanting to be Americans. They wanted to learn English and celebrate the Fourth of July and adapt themselves to our culture. During this process, our culture often picked up things from theirs and wove it into our fabric. That is what a melting pot is—a meshing and merging of disparate things to make something better. Today things seem very different. People are coming to this country to exploit our culture for their benefit with no desire to assimilate into our American way of life. This is a generalization, of course, but does seem to be more and more common. Many current immigrants seem to want the rest of us to adapt to their culture, language, and way of doing things. In other words, they don't want to change at all. It is like they want their own little country within ours. This phenomenon is potentially explosive and may at some point cause great divisions in our country. I personally know some resident aliens who have no desire to ever become American citizens, who work here only to make money to send overseas, who refuse to abandon any of their culture and have no wish to adopt any of ours, and who candidly admit that they don't even like the United States very much. They are "using" us for their own benefit, and that is the truth!

Is the above paragraph contradictory to what I said about the races and ethnic groups getting along? Not necessarily. Let me give an example. If a Chinese family moves next door to a white family but the families share similar values and traditions and cultures, the difference in races is likely to be of no matter. The values, traditions, or cultures don't have to be identical. But if their cultural mores are similar, the families are likely to get along. On the other hand, two

African-American families could live next to each other and if they did not share similar values, traditions, and cultures, they may well not get along. The point here is that it is not strictly a matter of race or ethnicity that unites or divides us. In fact, socio-economic differences are far more divisive in our society than racial differences. But a society has to have a somewhat common culture in order to thrive and survive. Many fear that we are becoming a series of little nations within one. If the cultural objectives, values, customs, and traditions of each of these little "nations" is too diverse, then friction and ultimately conflict will be the inevitable result. That is not to say that our culture is the best or anything like that, but, for better or worse, it is our culture, and we have a right to expect that people living in this country at least respect and honor our cultural mores. Is this being xenophobic? To some extent—maybe. But it is directed only at those who have come to exploit and use us and who have no desire to assimilate themselves into the American culture and way of life. In some ways, recent immigration to the United States has really been more like an invasion. It should be noted that the United States is not the only country facing this issue. Many of the countries in Europe are facing the exact same problem.

Is there a solution? Maybe we could start by limiting the number of foreign workers we allow into this country. We could issue visas for a certain time limit, and with no extensions, and then spend some money enforcing the law in that regard, including forfeiture of all assets if you stay beyond your visa. We could give people who come to this country a certain time frame in which to apply for and become citizens. Maybe we should freeze immigration entirely for some specified period. Some suggest that we make English *the* national language and that all immigrants should have to pass a comprehensive written and oral exam in English to obtain citizenship. Unfortunately, this appears to be a problem with no optimal solution. What do you think?

Chapter 9

Can't We Just Agree to Disagree?

With such a huge population, with such religious diversity, racial diversity, ethnic diversity, economic diversity, educational diversity, and all the other diversities we have, uniformity about any decision or policy is *impossible!* Who is the only person in the universe that will agree with you about everything? You. As stated previously, every human being that has ever walked on the earth is unique from every other human being. The only person who will ever see all things exactly the same way as you is you. Therefore, disagreement is inevitable and unavoidable. That's the truth and we need to accept that. The key to survival of the human race is to learn how to disagree without killing each other.

I love sports, and in an ironic way, sports provide one model for how we could live our lives. Without steroids, though! When one team plays another, or even when individuals face off, the competitors try their very best to prevail. In contact sports, like football or rugby, it can get very rough, but the competitors are governed by rules to prevent unfairness or undue injury. What typically happens when the game or match is over? The opponents hug each other, say something like "good game," and start preparing for the next game. There is rarely any lingering animosity or hatred created. When a player does feel that way, teammates will try to calm him down because they know such feelings are counterproductive to the ultimate goals of the team. This concept of sports works really well, as it allows for vigorous competition but in a congenial, regulated way.

But what happens in the world outside sports when there is vigorous competition? Let's take the issue of abortion. The two different sides of this issue are both adamant in their respective beliefs, and both sides want to win in the legislative arena, the judicial arena, the executive arena, and the arena of public opinion. It is apparent that neither side is ever going to capitulate to the other. Game on! In playing the "game," both sides are entitled to espouse their particular viewpoints. The rules should be the rules of law that are there to prevent unfairness and injury. So what happens in this kind of a situation when there is no scoreboard or time clock and no definitive winner? Why don't you hug each other, say "good game," and move on? Here's the truth—the two sides in this issue are *never* going to agree or find some sort of mutual compromise. It just isn't going to happen. So why can't both sides just agree to disagree? Violence and hatred and Molotov cocktails aren't going to change anything. Each side is entitled to believe the way it wants to. Both sides are well meaning, but they view the world differently. Nothing is going to change that. Doesn't it make a lot more sense to accept that truth and move on? Sometimes others are going to see the world differently than you. Right or wrong here is clearly a matter of perspective, so much so that right and wrong are really irrelevant. The truth is that people see things differently and therefore are going to have disagreements. And that is okay. It is not only okay, it is absolutely unavoidable. So why not accept it instead of living our lives getting frustrated and angry and hateful because someone disagrees with us. Don't take things so personally. Just acknowledge that disagreement and move on. It really is okay. In fact, given the population of the world, on any one issue there are probably millions of people that disagree with you. I know that if anyone ever reads this manuscript, not one person will agree with everything I have said. Some will agree with a lot, some with a little, and some with none. And that's okay. I accept the truth that people have different views. As long as I respect you and allow you your views and you respect me and allow me my views, there is no need for physical conflict. Just because you see the world from a different perspective than I do doesn't make you bad or evil or an idiot. All it means is that you see things differently. Remember that no one, and I mean literally no one, sees the world the exact same way you do. No one ever has, and no one ever will. We are all unique and different, and therefore at some point you are going to have to agree to disagree with someone. Either that or you will have to wipe out the entirety of humanity so no one will ever disagree with you. *Here is the most important truth of all—you can never force anyone to see things exactly your way.* It is impossible to accomplish! To try is an exercise in futility and ultimately only results in human suffering, degradation, misery, and needless death. The world would be a far, far better place if we could all just agree to disagree civilly and respectfully. Just like in sports, sometimes you'll win and sometimes you'll lose, and either way, if you say "good game" and move on to the next issue in your life, you will be a much better person for it. There are two very, very old maxims that would make us much happier if we could only remember and live by them: Do unto others as you would have them do unto you; and live and let live.

Chapter 10

The Truth about Evil

Now that everyone is feeling all warm and fuzzy (and hopeful?), there is a need to throw in some sobering reality. There is evil in the world and there always will be. In fact, there needs to be evil. Why? If you lived in a place where all the weather variables (like temperature, humidity, wind, etc.) were exactly the same every day, the concept of a hot day or a cold day would be unknown to you. If every person had the exact same personality and mood all the time, you would never know happy or sad, angry or friendly, or any other emotion. Fortunately, our world is made up of contrasts. The concept of "happy" is meaningless without something to contrast it to. So it is that the concept of "good" would not exist without the contrast of "evil." Every philosophy and religion that I have ever heard of acknowledges these opposing forces. You can't truly experience something without having something else to contrast or compare it to, and that is why in order to have "good" we also need to have "evil."

What is good? What is evil? It is obvious that these concepts will always be extremely subjective, varying depending on each individual's perceptions. In Neale Donald Walsch's *Conversations With God* books, the author suggests that there are only two basic human emotions—love and fear. All other emotions are derivatives of either love or fear. This makes sense and rings true. Therefore, "good" can be defined as something motivated by love or some derivative of love, like compassion, sympathy, understanding, empathy, etc. "Evil" can be defined as something motivated by fear or some derivative of fear like jealousy, envy, hatred, etc. Those who try to do the right thing for the right reasons would normally be considered "good." Those who do the wrong thing for the wrong reasons would normally be considered "evil." And there is the vast middle ground of those doing the wrong thing for the right reasons and those doing the right thing for the wrong reasons. It is in that middle ground where the concepts of good and evil get to be very subjective and reasonable people may legitimately disagree.

In my experience, human actions have always consisted of a broad spectrum of conduct. Generally, there are actions that almost all people would agree are "good" and actions that almost all people would agree are "evil." For example, if a four-year-old girl is lost in a snowstorm, taking the child to a safe, warm place until the parents can be found would pretty much universally be looked upon as being a "good" thing to do. In contrast, kidnapping, raping, and murdering that same four-year-old girl would, I think, be universally looked upon as being an "evil" act. But, of course, the world is not that simple. There are an infinite number of acts that might have been taken that are between the two extremes. And whether any act taken is deemed to be "good" or "evil" would depend on each person's values and morals. Let's say a teenage boy found the little girl, took her to his house, undressed her, and gave her a hot bath before calling the authorities. To some, this might be a perfectly acceptable and "good" thing to do. To others, this would be totally inappropriate and "evil" conduct. The point here is that we all need to recognize that "evil" does exist in the world, but we also need to recognize that when you take away the extremes, good and evil become amorphous concepts that will vary depending on each person's unique view of life. To reiterate what I have been trying to emphasize, no one will see good and evil the exact same way that you do. We are all unique and that is okay!

Let us discuss the far end of the spectrum that I will call extreme evil. Perhaps being in law enforcement for over thirty-two years has made me biased, but my truth is that there are some people in society who live their lives at the far end of the spectrum in the place we would pretty much all call evil. It is doubtful that anyone acts in an evil manner one hundred percent of the time, but there are those in the world who could walk into a class of kindergartners and kill every living soul and then go home and take a nap. This is a hard concept for some people to accept. Many do not want to believe that such evil actually exists, despite all the current and historical evidence to the contrary. But it does, and we as a society need to recognize it and deal with it accordingly. Despite what some want us to believe, not every person can be rehabilitated or saved. The truth is that there are some very evil people in our society who will continue to engage in "extreme evil" acts unless they are forcibly segregated from the rest of us and confined. We can debate how best to accomplish this segregation—be it life in prison or the death penalty. How we accomplish the segregation is less important than society's acknowledgment of the need to do something and then the will to do it. It seems that we are far more tolerant of extreme acts of misconduct than we used to be. We tend to want to cast everything in that middle ground between the extremes on the spectrum of good and evil. In some ways, it is as if we are afraid to acknowledge that "extreme evil" even exists. It is certainly true that along that good-evil spectrum there is no clear-cut dividing line between the extremes and the sliding scale of the middle ground. Some acts are going to result in legitimate disagreement as to how to categorize the conduct. But come on! Kidnapping, raping, and killing a child? Walking into a school, business, or shopping mall and gunning down innocent people? How about Bernie Madoff and all the destruction he caused? Yes—even white-collar criminals can commit acts of "extreme evil." White-collar criminals "destroy" far more lives in this country than murderers do, and unlike a lot of murders where the perpetrator is in a highly emotional state, white-collar crimes are calculated, planned, and coldly executed.

The point in all of this is to get us as a society to get our collective heads out of the sand and recognize that there is true evil among us. That level of evil is always going to exist. No program or rehabilitation effort is ever going to change it or cure it, so let us acknowledge the truth and deal with it effectively, directly, and swiftly. Let's define the extremes that are totally unacceptable to us as a society. Let's decide as a people how we are going to deal with these people. In this matter, it will probably have to be a case of majority rules. And let's stop feeling sorry for these offenders and swiftly and permanently segregate these people from us one way or another. We will never stop evil from existing, but we can do a much better job of protecting the rest of us from the real evildoers.

Epilogue

I am sixty years old and have lived all throughout the United States. For whatever reason, I have always been interested in how and why people do things. The more people I got to know and talked to, the more I found out that each person has a public and private persona. In a one-on-one conversation, various "truths" are acknowledged, and, surprisingly, there is not a lot of disagreement. But publicly, I guess because of fear of recrimination, ridicule, or a lack of confidence, people will often talk and act differently than they really feel. Hence, the elephants in the room that most of us know are there but that few of us will publicly acknowledge. Unfortunately, with the emphasis on political correctness, no matter how well motivated, the *de facto* effect is that many people are afraid to be open and honest about how they truly feel about things. We tend to create a false reality where we pretend something is true even though we know that the true reality is something else. Let me give an example. When I was a prosecutor, I handled, among a lot of other things, Department of Fish and Game cases. The department was having a lot of trouble with people gill-net fishing in the San Francisco Bay, so we all pretended that we did not do racial profiling. But the truth was that every single gill-netter ever caught by the department was Vietnamese, so if, at two a.m., a loaded pickup truck was leaving a known gill-net fishing area and the occupants appeared to be Asian, you'd have to be stupid not to suspect that they might have been involved in illegal gill-net fishing. Everyone knows what is probably going on. But we had to pretend that we didn't and justify a traffic stop on a broken taillight. Wouldn't we all be better off if we could just acknowledge and deal with the truth? How can we really make social progress as a species if we create these false "realities" and ignore the truth that we admit privately but deny publicly? The truth is the truth and it isn't going to change because we ignore it. Dealing with falsities, pretending they are truths, will never really get us anywhere. I hope by my words I will inspire more people to acknowledge publicly what they really believe privately. Let's all tell it like it is and then let the chips fall where they may. It drives me nuts to see some eighty-year-old white lady from Iowa being practically strip searched at the airport security checkpoint! Come on! How many old white ladies from Iowa have committed terrorist attacks? We know that the terrorists who are the big threats are Middle Eastern Muslim fanatics. Why can't we just say that and deal with that truth? The truth is that I'd bet that every cop in America would tell you privately that in certain types of cases, racial profiling works. Yes—some people are going to be inconvenienced, but what about balancing an individual's inconvenience versus the greater good? We place so much emphasis on the individual that we tend to ignore the mass of individuals called the general public. It is like trying to save or protect a single tree but ignoring the overall health of the forest. Since we have not made much, if any, progress sociologically as a species over the last ten thousand plus years, why don't we try a different approach? Let's try talking about the elephants in the room. Let's try understanding that each of us is unique and that sometimes a majority of people might agree with your particular point of view and sometimes you may be the lone voice in the wind. And that is okay! No one is ever going to see the world exactly as you do. We need to learn how to disagree respectfully and civilly. Although as a society we always need to respect individual rights and views, as individuals we need to respect the general will and common good. The truth is that sometimes you'll "win" and sometimes you'll "lose" and that is just the way of life. We are supposed to admire and honor "truth" but the reality is that we often ignore it and hide from it. So whether you agree or disagree with my truths, let us all make a commitment to be open and honest about our own truths and yet be tolerant and understanding of others and their truths.